Chameleons

by Grace Hansen

ABDO
REPTILES
Kids

Visit us at www.abdopublishing.com

Published by Abdo Kids, a division of ABDO, P.O. Box 398166, Minneapolis, Minnesota 55439.

Printed in the United States of America, North Mankato, Minnesota.

032014

092014

PRINTED ON RECYCLED PAPER

Photo Credits: Getty Images, Shutterstock, Thinkstock
Production Contributors: Teddy Borth, Jennie Forsberg, Grace Hansen
Design Contributors: Dorothy Toth, Renée LaViolette, Laura Rask

Library of Congress Control Number: 2013952303
Cataloging-in-Publication Data
Hansen, Grace.
 Chameleons / Grace Hansen.
  p. cm. -- (Reptiles)
ISBN 978-1-62970-058-8 (lib. bdg.)
Includes bibliographical references and index.
1. Chameleons--Juvenile literature.   I. Title.
597.95--dc23
                    2013952303

Table of Contents

Chameleons

Chameleons are reptiles.

All reptiles have **scales**

and are **cold-blooded**.

5

Chameleons live in Africa, Asia, and Southern Europe. You can find them in **jungles** and **deserts**.

7

Chameleons come in many sizes. Some are as small as your fingernail. Others are as big as a cat!

9

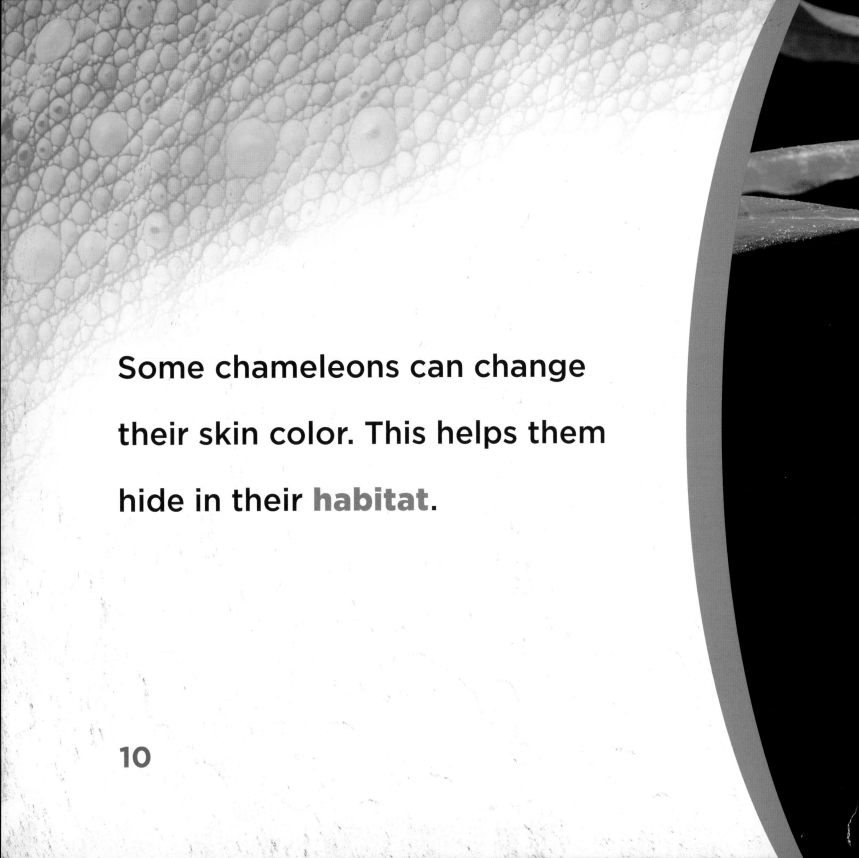

Some chameleons can change their skin color. This helps them hide in their **habitat**.

Chameleons have curled tails.
They wrap their tails around
branches. That keeps them safe.

Chameleons can look two different ways at once. They look for food and danger.

Food

Chameleons like to eat berries, leaves, and insects.

Chameleons' tongues are amazing. They use them to catch live food.

Baby Chameleons

Most chameleons lay eggs.
Young chameleons are on
their own after they **hatch**.

21

More Facts

- A chameleon's tongue can be as long as its body!

- Chameleons change their skin color to blend in. But they also change color to communicate with one another.

- There are about 160 different species of chameleon.

Glossary

cold-blooded – animals whose blood temperature depends on the temperature outside.

desert – a very dry, sandy area with little plant growth.

habitat – a place where a living thing is naturally found.

hatch – to be born from an egg.

jungle – land covered with a lot of trees and other plants.

scales – flat plates that form the outer covering of reptiles.

Index

abdokids.com

Use this code to log on to abdokids.com and access crafts, games, videos and more!

Abdo Kids Code:
RCK0588